To Maxine
Lovely to meet
you. Happy
Christmas
Sally Page.

Flower Shop
Messages

Sally Page

FANAHAN BOOKS

Text copyright © Sally Page 2010
Photography copyright © Sally Page 2010
Design & Layout copyright © Billy Kelly 2010

First published in 2010
Printed and bound in China by C&C Offset Printing

Also by Sally Page:
The Flower Shop - A Year in the Life of an English Country Flower Shop
The Flower Shop Christmas
Flower Shops & Friends
Flower Shop Secrets
and
The Flower Shop in Your Garden

A CIP catalogue record for this book is available from the British Library

ISBN: 978-0-9553779-6-9

For sales contact:
The Manning Partnership
6 The Old Dairy,
Melcombe Road,
Bath, BA2 3LR.
Telephone 0044 (0) 1225 478444
Fax 0044 (0) 1225 478440
E-mail sales@manning-partnership.co.uk
Distribution: Grantham Book Services

Published by Fanahan Books
Evelyn House, Leddington Way, Gillingham, Dorset, SP8 4FF
www.fanahanbooks.com

For Pippa Bell

(who I do love more than new shoes)

I have gathered a garland of other men's flowers and
nothing but the thread that binds them is my own

Michel Eyquem de Montaigne

Contents

Introduction

"My sister has been struck by lightning.". "Our goat has eaten our neighbours' hedge." "George has painted his Granny's hair green." As a florist you learn to take most things in your stride and it is not long before you realise that, when people are lost for words, flowers have a language all of their own.

One of the many joys of working as a florist, and photographing and writing my series of flower shop books, is that I have been fortunate enough to glimpse so many aspects of people's lives. A flower shop gives a unique window into the world of the community around it, and part of that world is illuminated by how flowers help people to express what sometimes seems inexpressible.

In this book I particularly want to recognise those flower buyers who do manage to find the right words. Their messages can be inspiring, at times funny and sometimes even sad. Amongst them, there will always be a few messages that leave you wondering (your head full of possibilities), what was that all about? It is true that florists have to be very discreet, but there is no rule to say they can't be nosey too!

I owe a huge thank you to the people who sent me their messages and to the many florists who helped me. These florists allowed me access to their gorgeous shops and beautiful flowers, and in many instances worked with me styling the shots I was taking. They kept me topped up with coffee and cake, and then sent me on my way with bundles of flowers.

And people wonder why I smile so much.

Sally Page

Beginnings & Birthdays

Whether you are embarking on the adventure of a new home, a new job, or even a new hip, flowers seem to me a wonderful way to mark the beginning of something. I can still remember some of the delicately fragranced posies I was sent when my daughters were first born. Including one thoughtful friend who waited a few weeks before sending anything, so that just when the last of the initial blooms had faded, a new bouquet arrived on my doorstep.

Sadly, these days few people buy me flowers. It seems that many are frightened of giving a florist the wrong thing. The other day a friend appeared on my doorstep saying "I nearly brought you flowers, but remembered just in time, so I have brought you sausages instead!"

It is not clear when the custom of communicating through flowers actually started. There are some records dating back to the 1400s of flowers being used to convey messages, but it is thought that it was in the early 1900s that greetings written on cards began to be regularly included with a delivery of flowers. In 1910 Henry Dudley was running a paper company in Michigan and he liked to include his own note when he sent his wife flowers. He cut out squares of paper for these messages and called into the local drugstore to buy the small envelopes normally used for pills. His company went on to produce these cards and envelopes and sell them to florists around America.

Happy New Year, may it bring you all you could wish for, health and happiness ...

and who knows, maybe that elusive single man

Surprise, Surprise
It's started!

To baby Abbie, the flowers in my garden did not believe me when I told them how beautiful you are, so I am sending you some so they can see for themselves

Thank you so much for delivering our lovely daughter Molly

To my clever and beautiful wife
Thank you for the most precious gift, our new son. I am so proud of you

Congratulations of the birth of your son
May all your troubles be little ones, unlike the baby who was huge!

To Harry, you have taught me so much already
Can I teach you to play football?

Love your Dad

Y ou're in!

Missing you already

M ay your roof never fall in and may you never fall out

A birthday without flowers is like a ship without a sail
Here is a sail for your ship

Fab at forty and always gorgeous

43 roses, one for every birthday misse
Love alway

Happy Birthday
Lots of love a silly stubborn old fool

Enjoy it
It only happens once
(On 80th birthday)

Fingers Crossed

There is nothing like observing the transformation of a customer who has been into the shop one week sending 'good luck' flowers, to seeing the same person a few weeks later when they call in to send a 'congratulations' bouquet. You feel their worry with them, and are almost as pleased as they are when they tell you their good news.

"She just phoned and said 'You are now speaking to *Doctor* Burrow'!"

Often in the background are friends and family watching over these worried customers; flowers are sent to a mum when her child goes on a gap year, a posy may be ordered for someone waiting anxiously for hospital tests, or a big bunch of tulips for a wife whose husband has decided it would be a good idea to run six marathons across the Sahara in six days. These all call for flower too.

Gipsies consider white heather a symbol of luck, whilst some Channel Islanders throw flowers on the water by your boat to bring you luck on your journey and to wish you a speedy and safe return.

I'd say break a leg, but they are such lovely legs

Go n-éirí an bóthar leat
Irish blessing for a journey: 'May the road rise to meet you')

Good Luck, have fun, but come back soon or the frog gets it!

I got the job!

    You get the flowers

Carpe Diem

W ell done Smelly, I knew you could do it

Amazing!
ove from The Drunk

A star for my little star
(On losing weight)

Y ou're blooming brilliant!

Good friends are like stars, you don't always see them but you know
they are there. Well done from all of us

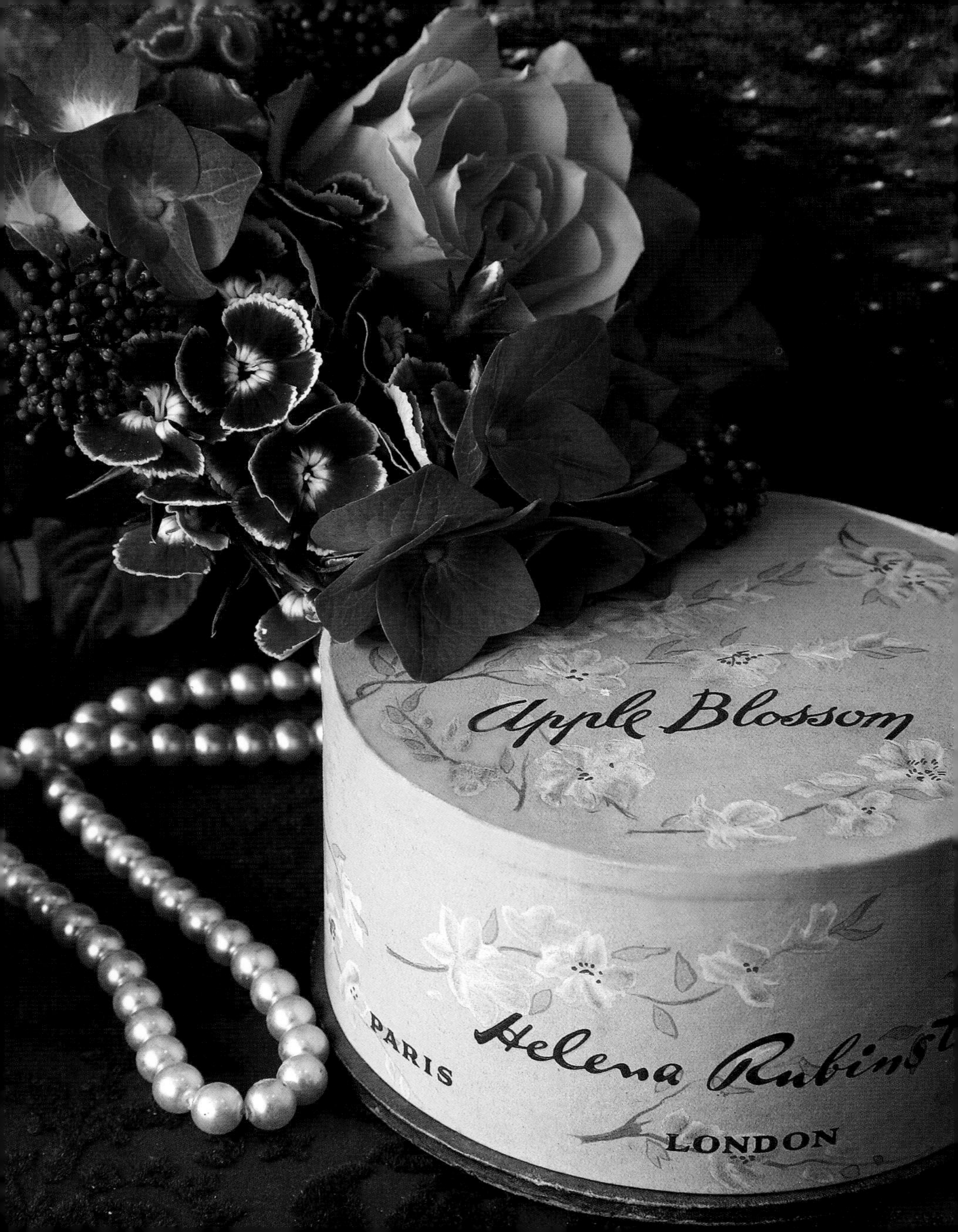
Apple Blossom
PARIS
LONDON

My Mum

How do you thank someone for bringing you into the world? For feeding you, teaching you vital life skills (like how to bake cupcakes and the words to ABBA songs), for chasing away nightmares and hugging you when you're sad, and for loving you no matter what mistakes you have made, whatever your hair is doing that day, and despite all your flaws?

There are more than 400,000 words in the English language, yet there still don't seem to be quite enough to say what you really want (and really should) to your mum. There are some things that you can only really say with flowers.

To me, the enduring link between mums and flowers shows itself year after year on Mothers' Day. Around the country children flock to flower shops to buy something for their mum. Children who cannot see above the counter exchange sweaty coins for a posy for Mummy, whilst big children send cards and blooms from university, or come down to visit with a jug of flowers and their own children in tow.

In this book my mum discusses the historic meanings of flowers, and the often complex associations they can embody. However for me, the meanings are often much more simple, and personal. When thinking about my mum and flowers, there are a few in particular that spring to mind. Tulips that are as elegant as she is, full-blown peonies that look as soft as one of her hugs and really sunflowers, because as one of the messages reads, "You are the one the sun shines for."

We may never be able to find the exact words, but a heartfelt message and a beautiful bouquet can often speak more than novels. One of my favourite quotes my mum has found for this book is short, and simple. "I love you very much Mummy." Because that, and some glorious flowers, says it all really.

Libby Page

To Mum, for keeping secrets, promises and your temper

Mum, what I would like to be able to give you most of all is time to rela

I know we don't always see eye to eye, but I do love you

I love you very much Mummy

Thanks a bunch top Mum

Mummy, Nipper and I are sorry we ate all your chocolates

To Il Capitano, from your loving husband
and all your delightfully behaved children

You are the light beneath my door

You are the one the sun shines for

And not forgetting Grandmas ...

Nan, thank you for my first birthday party
A fantastic cake and the best pass the parcel

To Mum (and now, Granny)
Now I understand!
Thank you

Saying Thank You & Sorry

he Victorians developed a whole language of flowers with different varieties ommunicating complex, and at times, contradictory meanings - depending 1 which flower language book you were using. The idea was originally rought to England by Lady Mary Wortley Montague via her letters written om the Turkish Embassy in the 1700s, in which she explained how objects ich as flowers, stones and feathers had symbolic significance.

any of the meanings the Victorians adopted were rooted in love messages, ith wonderful interpretations, such as, her smile is the soul of witchery (red elargonium), speak low if you speak love (King Charles rose), and, you are ch in attractions (ranunculus). However you would want to be careful of cluding any persimmon plant your offering as this meant, iry me amidst nature's eauty.

sing this language of flowers decide that I would much ther someone was trying say thank you to me than orry. In the former I might ceive a bouquet of full blown ses or camelias, where as morse was symbolised by ispberries.

here are no end to the thank ous and sorrys that a florist ill encounter in their life – id just when you think that ou have heard them all, meone will send flowers thank a friend for lending iem her husband (I think r DIY) or will apologise for urping over coffee many ears ago!

A small token for a very big thank you

Thank you for everything. Words are not enough

Thank you for the painting, the company and the advice

A thousand thank yous for helping with the chaos

Thank you for helping turn me into Cinderella
You are definitely not an ugly sister!

Let us be grateful to the people who make us happy;
they are the charming gardeners who make our souls blossom

Thanks for the cottage. You saved my life

I am so sorry I sat on your hat

Sorry for spoiling what was a lovely evening
and thank you for being so kind and forgiving

Oops! All my love

Sorry about muddy eek and squeek, with lots of lov

I'm sorry for shocking you. Thanks for looking after me
I don't remember!

Ok, ok, ok, you were right ... again!

Sorry for being me

I'm sorry my duck ate your washing

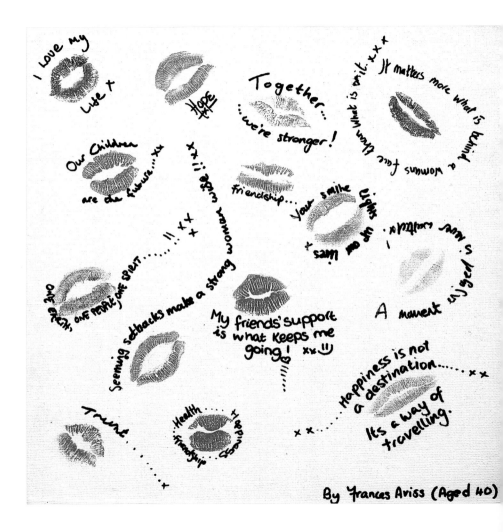

Being There

I once read that 85% of flower deliveries are sent from women to women. I can easily believe this. Many of the ladies I meet coming into flower shops seem to be thinking about their girlfriends, their mums, their sisters, their daughters. They remember dates that are important to them, they worry if they are worried and they rejoice when they are happy. And standing amongst the flowers, watching all this going on around me, I think it is one of the best things about being a woman.

I recently organised a fund-raiser for Rwandan charity, Msaada. I gave local people canvases and asked them to paint a picture, which we then auctioned. In all, over a hundred painters took part, most of whom were complete beginners. One mother and daughter decided to invite their girlfriends around and, wearing bright lipsticks, asked them all to kiss their canvases and write a message. They wanted to symbolise how Rwandan women have supported each other; women helping women. Something that I believe is going on all over the world, including in a small way in our flower shops.

W̶e̶ heard you were feeling blue

My door and wine are always open

*F*or when you're
feeling sad

Just remember, he ate garlic and hated ABBA

eep smiling darling, surely there are still a few decent fish in the sea

Lots of love Big Sis

For lovely Donna, You see sometimes nice things do happen

Flowers; putting Prozac in the shade!

I'm on my way

You may be losing your hair, but you will never lose your sparkle
With love from us all

I hope these flowers bring some brightness to your sleepy da
I can't wait to see your special self back on form soo

Some big ass flowers to cheer you!

If anyone can crack this, you can

For some moments in life
there are no words

Dear Granny we are glad to hear you are feeling better
Please don't go up any more ladders

It takes both sunshine and rain to make a rainbow
                              Get well soon Mummy

When we said 'break a leg', we didn't really mean it!

Love You

am pointedly ignoring
ne men who continually
ll me "I can't send her
owers, she will think I
ave done something
rong", I am brushing
side those who send
essages such as
'hese flowers cost me
12.95" and I am not
ven going to glance
those who will insist
n writing things like,
Desperate? Lonely? Be
y Valentine."

stead I want to
pplaud those men
nd women) who
ave romance coursing
rough their souls
id who are not afraid
say it with flowers.

eople who remember a favourite flower, who understand how lovely it is
see that the bouquet arriving at the reception desk is for you, and who
ccasionally send flowers to a loved one - just because.

s early as the Ottoman Empire flowers were used as a symbol of love. Within
e restricted communities of the harem silent messages could be sent to
otential lovers. An iris symbolised 'no' where as muscari meant 'yes'. Later
is symbolism was copied by the Victorians, and not only were flowers
ven specific meanings, but the way they were dressed and handled had
gnificance too. For example, when flowers were given, if the hand or ribbon
as inclined to the left it meant 'I', if it was to the right it signified 'thou'.

It has always been you

To Beautiful ... lucky me,
love from Ugly

Monstrously yours!

Kiss me Kate!

You are the fairest

B_{ig} WOW 50!
Your still secret, still admirer

I may be 11,000 miles away and 25 years too late,
but you still make me smile

Because I will always love you

To Mouse, love Badger

Flowers now – fireworks later

Love Buttons x

Marry me!

Home is not home
without you

If I had a single flower for every time I thought of you, I could walk forever in my garden

To the Queen of beekeeping, from the Big Beast

Can you believe it is only 12 years?
Counting the 27 days until I am home again.
Cannot wait until I am in your arms

Just love your rigging, the cut of your jib
Your curving sails and jaunty rib
Come shiver my timbers, pipe me aboard
Let's go below and discover your hoard

I would climb mountains and slay dragons

To Richard, that rare person who understands silence

Happy 6 years and 5 months

Life is still getting better thanks to you
(and so is the garden!)

Happy Anniversary, 17 years and still going strong
Some people get less for murder!

Always have
Always will

Grow old along with me, the best is yet to be

My Love, My Life, My Wife
                    45 years and still My Love

Will you still love me, when I'm sixty-four?

Saying Goodbye

or many years flowers have been associated with funerals and remembrance; ondoners hung white wreaths on lamp posts when Queen Victoria died, oppies became a poignant symbol of the wild flowers growing on the evastated fields of Flanders, and, more recently, public grief at the death of rincess Diana was eloquently expressed through floral tributes.

s a florist there are times hen you feel achingly adequate in the face of omeone's grief, but it is lways a privilege to be here, doing the little that ou can to help. Whether is creating a wreath of inter vegetables for a een gardener's funeral, dding an olive branch o some flowers where here has been a difficult amily relationship, or lanting up simple and elicate snowdrops for a rave.

To everything there is a season, and a time to every purpose under heaven: a time to be born and a time to die; a time to plant and a time to pluck up that which is planted ...

Ecclesiastes

Memory is a golden chain that binds us until we meet again

To Dad, Thank you. Without you this geek wouldn't be here

With fond memories of summer evenings on the cricket pitch

To 'the master of the revels'
Simply a legend

You will be dearly missed as our Nanny,
Great Nanny and 'old, old Nana'

Thank you Mam for the great journey of life ...I will make you proud!

Thank you for listening

Have fun in heaven!

You were right, your bark was far worse than your bite.
God bless

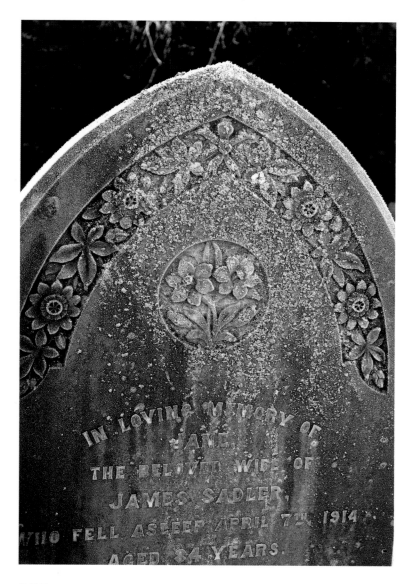

We never managed to change the world,
but you made a darn good job of just being part of it

So very patient. Such painful playing. You were a wonderful teacher

Everytime we say goodbye

You walked beside me through the roses and the rain

Do not cry because it is over. Smile because it happened

And Finally

There were so many occasions and messages that, sadly, could not fit into this book. I would have gladly gone on gathering messages and flowers, meeting more florists and visiting more flower shops; but I had to stop somewhere.

But before I go, I have included a few final messages that either left me staring into space ... wondering, or that just made me smile.

I hope very much that the flowers and messages in this book have made you smile too. If they have, then my job is done.

Sally Page

I still don't believe it!

D. L. E. S. A. B.
2 K. T.

You can keep it as a reminder of me

Happy Tuesday

Yes!

Love life and deckchairs

I'm not a grumpy old man

Happy Christmas Lovely Lady

Merry Christmas and thank you for the fish

Thank yous

Becky Macnab, The Potting Shed Florist. Tel: 07919 173707
becky@pottingshedflorist.co.uk
(Photos on pages: 34, 37, 39, 84, 110)

Café des Fleurs
Unit 2, Corn Exchange, Strand Quay, Rye, East Sussex. TN31 7DB
Tel: 01797 227894
www.cafedesfleurs.co.uk
(Photos on pages: 13, 33, 43, 72, 73, 96, 98, 125)

Garden Inn
Forsight House, High Street, Stockbridge, Hampshire. SO20 6HF
Tel: 01264 811 661
www.garden-inn.co.uk
(Photo on page: 20)

Green Pavilion
6 Terrace Road, Buxton, Derbyshire. SK17 6DR Tel: 01298 77309
(Photos on pages: 59, 70, 81, 107)

Hedge Rose
Sonia Wright Plants, Buckerfields Nursery, Ogbourne St George, Nr Marlborough,
Wiltshire. SN8 1SG Tel: 01672 841217
www.hedgeroseflorist.co.uk
(Photos on pages: 8, 15, 46, 47, 111)

Knighton Flowers
205 Clarendon Park Road, Leicester. LE2 3AN Tel: 0116 270 6767
www.knightonflowers.co.uk
(Photos on pages: 6, 7, 11, 36, 57, 97)

Patricia Knowles Florist
1 Upper Church Street, Farnham, Surrey. GU9 7PW Tel: 01252 715597
www.patriciaknowles.co.uk
(Photo on pages: 6, 94)

Spriggs
Lancaster House, Golden Square, Petworth, West Sussex. GU28 0AP
Tel: 01798 343372
www.spriggs-florist.co.uk
(Photo on pages: 82, 83)

Ted Martin Flowers
The Square, Tisbury, Wiltshire. SP3 6JP Tel: 01747 871333
www.tedmartinflowers.co.uk
(Photos on pages: 25, 29, 49, 50, 62, 66, 78, 79)

The Poundbury Florist
Lydgate Street, Poundbury, Dorchester, Dorset. DT1 3SJ Tel: 01305 268878
www.poundburyflorist.co.uk
(Photos on pages: 4, 12, 99, 101, 118, 119, 120)

VAAS
20 – 22 Heathcoat Street, Hockley, Nottingham. NG1 3AA Tel: 0115 959 8959
www.vaas.co.uk
(Photos on pages: 86, 87)

Wild Paeony
17 High Street, Shaftesbury, Dorset. SP7 8JE Tel: 01747 852662
www.wildpaeony.co.uk
(Photos on pages: 10, 41, 60, 61, 65)

Keri Harvey The Florist
Ayres Yard, Station Road, Wallingford, Oxfordshire. OX10 0JZ
Tel: 01491 838005
www.wallingfordflowers.co.uk

The Flower House
High Street, Mayfield, East Sussex, TN20 6AB Tel: 01435 873984
www.theflowerhouse.biz

The Flower Shop
102 High Street, Bushey, Hertfordshire. WD23 3DE Tel: 020 8950 3384
www.theflowershop.uk.net

I believe that a few people quoted from poems or books. These are: Pg 55 (Proust) Pg 102 (Robert Browning) and Pg 117 (Dr Seuss). I apologise if any others have slipped through unnoticed.

Also published by Fanahan Books:

THE FLOWER SHOP
A YEAR IN THE LIFE OF AN ENGLISH COUNTRY FLOWER SHOP

By Sally Page

FLOWER SHOPS
& friends
A YEAR'S JOURNEY AROUND ENGLISH FLOWER SHOPS

By Sally Page

THE FLOWER SHOP
Christmas
CHRISTMAS IN AN ENGLISH COUNTRY FLOWER SHOP

By Sally Page

THE FLOWER SHOP
in Your Garden
MAKING THE MOST OF THE FLOWERS AND FOLIAGE IN YOUR GARDEN

By Sally Page

FLOWER SHOP
Secrets

By Sally Page

For full details visit:
www.fanahanbooks.com